FROM THE CRADLE TO THE GRAVE

DR. ERNEST BRANCH

COVER ILLUSTRATED BY MACEO BRANCH

ISBN 978-1-64670-114-8 (Paperback)
ISBN 978-1-64670-115-5 (Digital)

Covenant Books, Inc.
11661 Hwy 707
Murrells Inlet, SC 29576
www.covenantbooks.com

T his book shall focus on the transformation of world information into Christ-centered living through the scriptures in the Bible. In the past, ministers of the Gospel of Jesus Christ were focused on the symptoms not the causes of unrighteousness.

Matthew 10:33–38 states, "Think not that I am come to send peace on earth: I came not to send peace, but a sword. For I am come to set a man at variance against his father, and the daughter against her mother, and the daughter in law against her mother in law. And a man's foes shall be they of his own household. He that loveth father or mother more than me is not worthy of me: and he that loveth son or daughter more than me is not worthy of me."

These scriptures are preparing the followers of Jesus Christ to be aware of humanity's perverted priorities, which is developed through the constant contact and expectations of family and friends. Consideration and love of God is not first.

Familial relationship and the satisfaction of the flesh became the highest priority. The desire for Christian education is derived through a Christ-centered family or friends who have been exposed to Godly information and wishes for a new lifestyle.

Royce Money states, "Through the family, God help us grow and mature, preparing us for lifelong fruitful roles in society. Through the family, God blesses others. The breakdown of traditional family patterns has been hastened by declining moral values" (3).

Money further reports that people are more concerned about themselves and what's in it for me than keeping the integrity of the family function.

Dr. Josh Moody comments on the family: "Christian experiences is too often influenced by our circumstances. When we are up God is great. When we are down God is distant. If things go our way, we have much to praise God. If times come that would test our patience we are tempted to give up. The Bible is one that is God-centered, not us-centered, or me-centered" (11).

Moody states that God always comes first and is the heart of life. God influences and invades all of reality. Moody reports that his happiness does not depend on his personal experiences but on God's love, grace, and mercy.

The Bible in Matthew 6:8 and 32 mentioned, "Be not ye therefore like unto them: for your Father knoweth what things ye have need of before ye ask Him." To mention the same concern in the same chapter emphasizes the desire of God to provide complete assistance to humanity. Humanity must learn biblical teachings and become obedient an student to the written word of God.

According to Carl Rogers, "Learning involves a change in one's self-perception. Significant learning takes place when self-initiation, personal responsibility, activity and relevance are present in the teaching-learning process" (113). Both Abraham Maslow and Carl Rogers report that "the highest priority is self-actualization for each individual." All Bible references in this paper come from the King James Version of the Bible, except where clearly noted by the student."

Abraham Maslow states that "individual deficiency needs (survival, safety, belonging, and self-esteem) must be met before they will be motivated to fulfill being needs (intellectual, achievement, aesthetic experiences, self-actualization, or reaching one's full potential)" (112). Maslow is best known for his theory of motivation based on a hierarchy needs over other concepts of educational attainment.

I agree with Maslow's concept of individual needs determining the priorities in people's lifestyle. A close examination of time management indicates that days are divided into three segments in order to provide for the basic survival needs of a consumer. Eight of those hours provide a consumer with the ability to pay for food, clothing, housing, and transportation. This the financial segment.

The next segment is consumed with in-home care services that provide food preparation, house cleaning, child-care/management, clothing readiness, financial management and bill paying, and finally, maintenance and housing upkeep and repair.

The time management approach for the final eight hour segment includes recreation, sleep and recovery but often has insufficient time to spend in God's Word. Stephen Covey states "The time management approach should become a habit intended to help a person achieve effectiveness in each segment including time spent in the Word of God" (6).

One needs to focus on the priorities of time management. Very little is a concern to the obedience to the Word of God. There are 168 hours in a week, and the average person only spends approximately ten hours trained in the Word of God. With this much worldly needs, it becomes very difficult for any other information to be of major concern. The daily obligation and lifestyles occupy most of the time in people's lives.

Let's examine how spiritual sickness began and how it developed from helplessness and dependence on others such as the main caregiver, who is usually a mother, to where it is today. When a child is born, it leaves the comforting temperature of the mother into a shocking exterior environment. The baby starts crying or is induced to cry from a slap on their bottom, encouraging it to cry.

This uncomfortable world causes stress to the newborn until a caretaker provides the necessary comfort by tending to the newborn needs. Cleaning the infant and surrounding it in a soft, warm blanket then placed on the warm body of the mother reduces the baby's stress. Should complications exist, special care and attention will aid the newborn with survival.

These initial encounters with the world is the beginning of dependence developed to assist the newborn with survival training other than the normal functions of nature. Dependence removes personal abilities to make decisions pertaining to lifestyles. It further neutralizes individual growth and development.

An inordinate amount of time is spent in life living through the expectations of others in order to confirm or legitimize ones' personality and expectations in life. Temporary gratification from other people is just that, temporary. This becomes a way of life because of the repetitions of dependent behavior.

There will come a time when individuals will have to make decisions that will empower them toward independent thinking. Independent thinking and learning encourage learners to be empowered through spiritual information from the Bible. Learners can act freely with other independent thinkers and interdependence can prevail. Without independent thinking, it is very difficult to have a personal relationship with God.

The provider of world information is more of a concern of health and welfare of the newborn with information to survive in the natural world not the spiritual world of God. If the family is not demonstrating Christ-centered behavior the chances are that they don't have a personal relationship with God. The lack of Godly information prevents the acquisition of Godly knowledge. Knowledge that is necessary to worship God in spirit and truth.

The combination of world information overrides the desire to live a Christ-centered life. The righteousness of God cannot manifest itself unless biblical information is taught, received, and understood. Consistent Godly information will provide appropriate development required to enhance acquisition of new information.

During the learning process, world rules and regulation will continue to establish the priority for the people of God because of the lack of biblical knowledge. A young man confessed to me and stated that "God made me and although I am alcoholic, obese, and taking thirty-three different medication. I thought I was alright. My doctor told me that I was killing myself, realized the spirit of God agreed with the doctor and I turned to God for help."

The man had reached six hundred pounds and was dying when he decided to get a stomach operation and seek, God and presently, he is under three hundred pounds. This man decided to be aware and follow the teaching of the Bible and satisfy God more than God's creations. His dependence on others to comfort and mask his sickness was removed.

The insertion of dependence of others is the beginning of dependence, shaping personality which leads to perverted priorities in establishing a personal relationship with God. The focus of world dominated information decreases the opportunity to excel in spiritual growth and development.

Once the parents become involved with the sharing of information, there is a possibility of delayed spiritual growth and development of the newborn. The family lifestyle may slow down the opportunity for new birth to break the dependence on world information rather than Godly information.

A newborn shows a great amount of independence by not having to call for assistance in their own way and eating without being taught and eliminating waste from their system without any outside assistance. When additional assistance is required, such as cleaning the waste of the newborn, providing proper nutritional food, and physical comfort the independent chain is broken or modified at the mercy of others.

There is still signs of independence because the newborn does not need to be shown how to hold the bottle and feed themselves and is able to signal when help or assistance is needed. This form of behavior or notification is not learned but instinct and demonstrates independent behavior.

The first encounter with learning new information should be focused on biblical information while demonstrating the Christ-centered life and independence starting with walking, using the bathroom, and keeping their clothing intact.

There will be a time when it becomes necessary for learners to move from independence to interdependence with other learners in order to continue the pursuit of additional information with other learners. This new information may come from their own personal experience in the world with additional information from the Christian environment.

A vital area of concern is the dependency of other people to determine capability and personality. Honesty occurs when the learner provides validation of themselves and not depend on friends and family members permission to acquire the virtues of intimacy and honesty with God.

Independent thinking and learning through the word of God leads to empowerment and developes a personal relationship with God and Jesus Christ.

The gathering at Christ-centered information centers, churches and through socialization with others, learners will be exposed to different mind-sets. These social events are very productive in establishing the basis of formulating a life journey through independent and interdependent thinking. Simultaneously, information about the world can be discussed with Godly information.

The learner must differentiate between useable and non-useable information. Although the facilitator of information may appear to be Christ-centered, the training of the learner is not guaranteed to receive much biblical knowledge.

The book of Romans, chapter 10:2 states, "For I bear them record that they have a zeal of God, but not according to knowledge. For they are being ignorant of God's righteousness and going about to establish their righteousness, have not submitted themselves unto the righteousness of God."

The Bible is saying that having the zeal for God does not guarantee the acquisition of Godly information and understanding. The overriding strength of world information neutralize the focus and desire for people to follow the teaching of Godly information.

The people have been accustomed to satisfy their physical needs because of the instant gratification and urgency to satisfaction of their need. This physical need urgency prohibits the desire to seek Godly information. World information dominates because the foundation of biblical information has not been established.

Righteousness training has not been received from Godly information; therefore, people went about establishing their own concept of Godly information and became zealous in thinking that their behavior was according to godliness.

Spiritual medicine not taken from the cabinet of God, demonstrating righteousness is the failure of the people to establish a personal relationship with God the Father, God the Son, and God the Holy Ghost. A personal relationship with the trinity of God can only be established through word of God from The Holy Bible.

Thus, the zeal for God does not guarantee the righteousness that is necessary for God to bless and answer prayers of his people. A personal relationship with God must be established through biblical information. A change of heart must prevail and exist. In disobedience to God, their expectations of compliance from God is not fulfilled.

A prayer is examined in the book of James, chapter 5:16: "The effectual fervent prayer of a righteous man availed much." Praying is very difficult when the understanding and desire to communicate with God in silence or verbally is not learned. It has been my experience that, unless praying instruction is taught and utilized on a regular basis, learners are not comfortable with speaking to God because they don't know God but know of God.

Communication with God through prayer is not the only means to establish a personal relationship. Music, dance, praise, song, singing, and worship services are very good opportunities for communicating with God.

Silent prayer is the most private and comfortable means of communication with God. God and God alone will have access to the conversation that contains very personal and private information dealing with a variety of issues and concerns.

Fear of self-disclosure is eliminated when speaking to God in prayer with truth and openness of the prayer. It is very important that the person praying develops comfort in sharing and spending enough time in prayer and communicating with God in order to establish a personal relationship.

The more time spent in prayer and communication with God will increase one's faith and confidence that God will not only hear but answer prayers. The repetition of prayer and Bible study helps a person develop a deeper trust of God and biblical understanding.

The effectiveness of the learning center is impacted by the environment of the learning site and the instructors. Regardless of whether the education being shared by family and friends is appropriate and useable, the environmental settings (physical as well as human interaction, students and instructors) all have an impact.

Albert Bandura states, "Individuals are products of environment shaping and also as a determent shaper of environment. One of the most significant results of his research is the theory of observational learning or modeling, which is learning by observation and imitating others. One supporting study has indicated that both hostile behavior and moral standards are readily imitated by observers" (109).

Many people teach the newborn irrelevant information or their personal experiences, which has not been productive to establish a Christ-centered lifestyle. Some of their experiences are useable, which may assist the newborn to cope the life journey in the new world of modern technology.

John Dewey states, "Learning must be practical and useable, concentrating on problem-solving and the contineous reconstruction of experiences"(112). Dewey states that the education of people must prepare them for the changing society which has to update information on a daily basis. If new information is not acquired and used indiviuals become nonproductive in society.

The Dewey concept of learning gives hope to older learners who need to transform world information into biblical uses. This method of information sharing is applicable to boot camp training where individuals' focus and concetration are applied to the acquisition of biblical information and understanding of the scripture for content and context.

Today, information is different. In many cases, it is immoral, sexually focused and greed and money motivated. Media control on dissemination via advertising on TV, cellular phones, and the Internet propagates demonic behavior, brainwashing ideology, and sinful behavior.

The level of education in a family is often recognized by abusive behavior, criminal activities, mental illness, or other abnormal behavior. This may assist the growth and development of spiritual sickness.

Students from preschool through college are measured to determine their ability to excel in basic learning skills, such as reading, writing, and mathematics. The test of successful education predicated on how we can regurgitate world information (dates and times) that will lead to employment, fame fortune and acceptance by the general population.

This recognition of who we are gives us substance, identity, and acceptance as a worthwhile person. Alfie Kohn gave an example of what a well-educated person may not represent the normal basic requirements which are not always a good representation of quality education.

Kohn stated that his wife, Alisa, graduated from Harvard University as a doctor of anthropology and later decided to go to medical school, and she became a medical doctor. He said that if anyone asked his wife what 8 times 7 is, she would panic because she never learned the multiplication table. Although his wife is well-educated according to her profession, she could not pass a math test" (2).

This gives society an opportunity to evaluate and analyze whether a different method of educating our young minds should be developed. The STEM program is what young minds have been introduced to keep up with the changing and growing technology that the world is presently operating.

The STEM web site states that the STEM education program reports, "The need to overhaul America's approach to teaching Science, Technology, Engineering, and Mathematics has launched an ambitious initiative to reverse our nation declined in these areas. Leaders in the education indicate the most important ingredient to success is the willingness to change."

The focus on modern technology appears to be developed out of fear and due to the power struggle that is taking place between God's creations and the devil. World power brokers are headed toward the extermination of humanity, not the preservation of God's creations.

The battles are not ours but the Lord. As stated in 2 Chronicles 20:15: "And He said, Hearken ye, all Judah, and ye inhabitants of

Jerusalem, and thou king Jehoshaphat, Thus said the Lord unto you, Be not afraid nor dismay by reason of great multitude; for the battle is not yours but God."

Some world information is important but in the book of 1 John, chapter 1:15, which states, "Love not the world, neither the things that are in the world. If any man loves the world, the love of the Father is not in him." What the scripture is saying is that people are more concerned with world events, prioritizing their focus on disobedient behavior rather than Godly obedience.

This world focus is counterproductive because book of Exodus, chapter 20 states, "Thou shalt have no other gods before me. Thou shalt not bow down thyself to them or serve them: for I the Lord thy God am a jealous God, visiting the iniquity of the fathers upon the children unto the third and fourth generation of them that hate me. And showing mercy upon thousand of them that love me and keep my commandments."

God don't want his people to worship or have any god before Him because He is a jealous God that will punish those who disobey Him. He further states that he will reward those who obey Him. Satan is waging a war to take over God's kingdom and the script today will continue to be written by the enemy of God.

To institute re-education, a new set of rules and regulations to transform useable world information into Christ-centered living must take place. The learner must acknowledge the spiritual sickness and seek help through Godly information in order to combat the difficulty of world information.

Spiritual healing can only happen when a new insertion of biblical information can penetrate the barriers that impede access to new information and a way of living. Learners must examine the necessity of a change of lifestyle to improve the quality of life through new information.

Spiritual sickness must identify and acknowledge the barriers to make the necessary changes. These barriers, once identified, can be reduced or eradicated through Christ-centered information. Unsatisfied wants or desires that causes spiritual illness because of the lack of biblical information will change behavior.

Spiritual sickness is masked and manifests into physical form through abnormal and self-destructive behavior, such as obesity, sexual immorality, profanity, drug and alcohol abuse, homosexuality, denial, isolation, idolatry, witchcraft, and hatred. These behaviors represent spiritual sickness as noted in the Bible.

The book of Galatians, chapter 5:19 states, "Now the works of the flesh are manifest, which are these: Adultery, fornication, uncleanness, lasciviousness. Works the complex mixture of evil desire and deed. The flesh is always active it never takes a vacation. Are manifest, plainly evident to everyone. These works all issue from a heart in rebellion against God and insisting upon doing as it will" (532).

Spiritual sickness was first produced in the Garden of Eden, where God's first human creations first exercised disobedience. Genesis 2:16–17 was the beginning of spiritual death: "And the Lord God commanded the man, saying, Of every tree of the garden thou mayest freely eat: But of the tree of the knowledge of good and evil, thou shalt not eat of it; for in the day that thou eatest thereof thou shalt surely die." God did not meant for humanity to experience physical death but spiritual death—spiritual death, not physical death that leads to spiritual sickness.

Spiritual sickness was activated after God had given humanity warnings concerning disobedience. The book of Genesis, chapter 3:6 states, "And when the woman saw that the tree was good for food and that it was pleasant to the eyes, and a tree to be desired to make one wise, she took of the fruit thereof, and did eat, and also gave unto her husband with her; and he did eat."

Satan's battlefield on earth demonstrates, that he is recruiting God's people to join the war in the Garden of Eden that started in heaven with God's angelic force. Revelation 12:7 states, "And there was war in Heaven; Michael and his angels fought against the dragon, and the dragon and his angels prevailed not; neither was their place found any more in heaven." This disobedient spirit still exists in the world, and the evidence of sin is all around us.

Once humanity executed disobedient, this one act of disobedience, God realize that he will always have difficulty with his human creation if the free choices of life remains. Jesus Christ work is being established to assist in the battle for the salvation of humanity against the prince of darkness.

The book of Isaiah, chapter 53:5 states, "But he was wounded for our transgressions, he was bruised for our iniquities, the chastisement of our peace was upon him, and with his stripes we are healed." This scripture is referencing the coming of Jesus Christ to take away the sins of the world. In the book of John, it reports that the word was God became flesh and dwelled among the people of God and they knew Him not because of their lack of Godly knowledge.

God wanted humanity to demonstrate Godly love through obedience to His wishes and desires. When obedience to God is not fulfilled, the opportunity to sin becomes a reality, and spiritual sickness manifests.

In Galatians 5:16, Paul realizes the struggle between the righteousness and unrighteousness that exist and writes, "This I say then; Walk in the Spirit and you shall not fulfil the lust of the flesh." The Bible says to worship God in spirit and truth, not flesh and blood, which can happen through the endorsement of Godly information.

Spiritual sickness occurs because of humanity's unrighteousness caused by humanity's disobedience to God's instructions. Genesis 3:17 states, "And unto Adam He said, Because thou hast hearkened unto the voice of thy wife, and hast eaten of the tree, of which I commanded thee, saying, Thou shalt not eat of it: cursed is the ground for thou sake; in sorrow shalt thou eat of it all the days of thy life."

Spiritual sickness punished God's creation. The humans became homeless with no place to live because God evicted humanity from the Garden of Eden. Genesis 3:22–24 states, "And the Lord God said, Behold, the man is become as one of us, to know good and evil: and now, lest he put forth his hand, and also take of the tree of life, and eat, and live forever: Therefore, the Lord God sent him forth from the Garden of Eden."

God constantly watches over, protects and disciplines His people. A demonstration of this was the eviction of Adam and Eve from the Garden of Eden due solely to their disobedience and not because He wanted to punish or reject his people. Humanity must learn to be obedient and receive the blessing from the creator of the heaven and earth.

After spritual sickness comes physical death, which can be prevent through biblical information. Develop a personal relationship with God through the teachings of God's words. Spiritual healing can eradicate or neutralize spiritual death through Christian education.

Christian education will provide the humanity with a new set of rules and regulations to guide their future behavior. John 15:3 states, "Now ye are clean through the word which I have spoken unto you." The word of God provides the necessary cleaning of unrighteousness and access to the blessing that Jesus Christ provided from His resurrection.

New information will be developed to assist with bringing the word of God to God's people. There are concerns about God not answering a prayer. As the Bible is explored, many of the stories that are presented in God's house of prayer are misrepresented, contaminated by improper understanding and lack of biblical knowledge.

In the book of Proverbs, chapter 1:28, it states, "Then shall they call upon me, but I will not answer; they shall seek me early, but they shall not find me; for that, they hated knowledge, and did not choose the fear of the Lord." The Bible continues to demonstrate many scriptures that supports the lack of response from God when prayer is not effective because the people has not been obedient to God's word.

The book of James, chapter 4:3 states, "Ye ask and receive not, because ye ask amiss, that ye may consume it upon your lust." In other words, God only responds to humanity when their heart is focused on obeying the will of God and His rules and regulations.

Bible boot camp was established to utilize a military type of learning environment where the military concept is used to encourage the student to a strict set of rules and regulation that will enhance biblical learning. In the classroom, all issues and concerns are directed and answered in the Bible, not the instructor.

The instructor shares biblical information that encourages the learners to focus and examine the information and decide whether information is useable or not. During the initial period of instruction, world information operates against the acquisition of Christ-centered information. Once the barrier has been discovered, the first area where the work for healing begins.

The various jargons used in business defines personal barriers relating to the factors that are personal to the sender and receiver and acts as a hindrance in the communication process. These factors include the life experiences, emotions, attitudes, behavior that hinders the ability of a person to communicate.

These barriers must be identified and removed to assist the learner's ability to acquire new information. There will be resistance to the necessary changes that will be taking place. Barriers can be identified as spiritual sickness. Spiritual sickness comes before physical death, which can be prevented through biblical information.

Developing a personal relationship with God through the teaching of God's words will lead to a new lifestyle. Christian education will provide the learners with a new set of rules and regulations that will guide their future behavior.

This method may enhance the learner's ability to use the Bible as their major source of information. The military type of training has been used since the beginning of civilization. The ability of trainees to receive and obey verbal and written information cannot be compared.

The *Webster* dictionary states that philosophy is a theory or attitude held by a person or organization that acts as a guiding principle for behavior. These thoughts impede growth and development and the acquisition of additional information. To be successful in acquiring current information, the purging of old information must take place.

The difficulty arises when learned behavior must be relearned or de-educated in order to reeducate and break through mind-sets. Reeducation, as stated in the *American Heritage Dictionary*, is "to instruct again, especially in order to change someone's behavior or belief. To retrain a person to function effectively; rehabilitate."

Full and honest disclosure of one's self in identifying events in life may cause one to hide in comfort zones. The neurosis, once identified by the individual, can be examined and processed for later consideration and work. Self-examination to determine the current status of successes and failures will help analyze the psychological status of the need for behavior modification. Self-actualization is the realization of a personal analysis of individual capabilities that are very important.

Many times, because of the masking and dishonesty, the learner becomes very defensive and refuses to identify with dysfunctional behavior or acts. They refuse to seek help because of the stigma that comes with the need for mental health intervention. The healing can begin once the dishonesty is recognized and accepted; then the healing process could begin.

Edward L. Hayes states that "Christian education implies in our contemporary world must somehow be subjected to the scrutiny of the explicit and implicit teachings of the scriptures. Viewing the Bible as God's living Word can recharge Christian education at its base" (31).

Lynn Gannett states that, in teaching for learning, "Christian educators are interested in change in an individual knowledge or behavior. Behaviorist exclusively emphasize change in behavior as the outcome of learning" (106).

Lawrence Richards said that the five level of learning maybe helpful for Christian educators:

1. Rote: ability to repeat without thought or meaning.
2. Recognition: ability to recognize biblical concepts.
3. Restatement: ability to express or relate concepts to biblical system of thought.
4. Relation: ability to relate Bible truths to life and see appropriate response.
5. Realization: actualizing response: to apply biblical truths in daily life (107).

Richards reported that "the goal of Christian education is to move learning to the level of realization. At this level change in the learner's behavior is more likely to occur" (107).

The book of Matthew, chapter 6:33 states, "But seek ye first the kingdom of God and his righteousness, and all these things shall be added unto you." Seeking God first allow humanity to establish a new set of rules and regulations for living. The Bible establishes a personal relationship through the Trinity to help His creations become obedient people.

The spiritual sickness of the learner's mind-set is developed over years of success and failure. The need for behavior modification is influenced by interacting with other people who share facets of the spiritual sickness. God still uses infirmed people to carry His message to His people for salvation, mercy, and grace. Comfort zones must be destroyed because they belong to Satan. The songster, Tasha Cobbs, sings "Break Every Chain" because she realizes chains are the works of the devil. Chains are any worldly information that interferes with nonbiblical training.

Breaking mind-sets and comfort zones will lead learners to new information from the Bible. The acquisition of this new biblical information become problematic when the learner resist change. Roy Zuck states, "Christian education is unique because of its subject matter-the Bible, God's written revelation; because of its goal-spiritual transformation of lives; and because of its spiritual dynamic—the work of the Holy Spirit" (107).

Zuck further states that "the Bible is not just information about God but God revealing Himself to His people. The goal of Christian education is that students know God and grow in Christlikeness. This is a transformation process. Students respond obediently to God's revelation" (108).

It appears that that many of the writings in Christian education is focused on young people where learning environments are institutionalized. Young learners are involved in formal schooling from preschool through college. An older follower of biblical learning is handicapped by organized church and world information systems.

Their denial of noncompliance to the scripture must be changed. The goal of Christian education must be emphasized in all age groups and taught with emphasis on the transformation to the word of God. Inclusiveness, not exclusiveness, should be considered when Godly information is shared.

John 20:21–22 states, "Then said Jesus to them again, Peace be unto you: as my Father hath sent me, even so, send I you, and when he had said this, he breathed on them, and saith unto them, Receive ye the Holy Ghost." When Jesus asks God to release the Holy Ghost to minister to God's people, many wonderful events began to unfold.

The lifestyle begins to operate differently, and through the study of the Bible, a vast change takes place. The blessing of God begins to flow like a waterfall, and the activities of the world are no longer important.

First John 2:15–16 states, "Love not the world neither the things that are in the world, if any man loves the world, the love of the Father is not in him. For all that is in the world, the lust of the flesh, and the lust of the eyes, and the pride of life is not of the Father but is of the world."

These scriptures demonstrate how spiritual sickness is caused by perverted priorities that takeover personal behavior and then that behavior becomes the gods of some people. Whatever occupies the focus of psychological way of life easily becomes the god whether worldly or biblical. Satanic forces are at work here to compromise God's people, so they denounce God. The word of God is the only tool that is available to ward off the attacks of the destructive forces of the devil.

The book of Job, chapter 1:6 states, "Now there was a day when the sons of God came to present themselves before the Lord, and Satan came also among them. And the Lord said unto Satan, whence comest thou? Then Satan answered the Lord and said, From going to and fro in the earth and from walking up and down in it."

This scene not only shows the relationship between God and Satan; even though Satan was evicted from heaven and banished to earth, they still communicate with each other. Satan, the fallen angel, still exists, and people need to realize the trickery of the devil. They need to remember that one third of the angelic force came to earth with Satan and still doing the will of the evil one.

In the book of John, chapter 14:16, it is stated, "And I will pray the Father, and he shall give you another Comforter, that he may abide with you forever. But the Comforter which is the Holy Ghost, whom the Father will send in my name, He shall teach you all things, and bring all things to your remembrance, whatsoever I have said unto you."

The word of God provides learners a storehouse of Godly information that will be released when attacked by the devil. The Holy Ghost drives God's human creation in a different direction; activities that were important are no longer important, and all types of activities, including dress codes, partying, dancing, nightclubbing, and even conversations have changed because holiness and righteousness dominate. Jesus's death and ressurection provided remission of sin's past, present, and future that people might have life in abundance. The influence of worldly information, education, and culture can develop a resistance that will not allow change to take place in the life of a learner.

Jeremiah 26:13 states, "Therefore amend your ways and your doing, and obey the voice of the Lord your God, and the Lord your God repent him of the of the evil that He hath pronounced against you."

This way of life becomes the basis or philosophy in how people live, and the psychology of this change can cause one to accept or reject this latest information that has been introduced. The basis will govern behavior and ability to allow change and innovative ideas to be learned and practice. Spiritual sickness still dominates the personality of the students in Bible boot camp.

Regardless of what reasons are used to implement a change in life, it can only happen if a strong desire for change is desired by God's people. Matthew 11:26 states, "Come unto me, all ye that labor and are heavy laden, and I will give you rest." The doors of salvation are always available if the desire for righteousness is paramount.

Matthew 5:6 states, "Blessed are they which do hunger and thirst after righteousness for they shall be filled." The inability to accept the Bible as a way of life is hidden in the definitions of spiritual sickness where confusion blocks one's ability to grasp the true meaning of the message of Jesus Christ's preaching.

Matthew 16:24 states, "Then said Jesus unto his disciples, if any man will come after me, let him deny himself, and take me up to his cross and follow me." Depending on one's self and others became a way to fulfill the immediate needs to sustain a good life.

The transferring of world information into biblical reality is a complicated transition that is predicated on time and understanding. Time spent in studying God's word needs to be increased to where an inordinate amount of time in our daily lives are dedicated to reading, study, listening, and understanding of the Bible.

It is possible that rote memorization can be effective in learning the words of God, but they believe that repetition is a more effective way to obtain and retain information. With enough time in studying the Bible, the word of God assists with the understanding and acceptance of God's word.

Here are comments from learners during class when asked to identify incidents that affected their relationship with God: "Where was God in my deepest need, that came from disappointment, abusiveness, rejections, lack of acceptance, lost loved ones, lost jobs, transportation, friends, food, clothing, shelter, hope, faith, trust, belief, medical assistance"(Galatian 5:22).

The present-day living triggers these negative events of the past into doubts that Godly love can prevail in one's life. These negative feeling need to be crucified on the Calvary cross with the resurrection power of Jesus Christ. If Jesus paid it all on the cross, why is the blessings from God all mighty missing in people's lives?

The word of God in the Bible has the medicine for all infirmities. The church is a spiritual hospital, and the Bible is the medicine cabinet where the healing power of God's word is available for no money but is not free. John 15:3 states, "Now ye are clean through the word which I have spoken unto you."

Jesus is recognized as the healing doctor with the power to perform miracles as shown in the book of Matthew, chapter 8 and the following verses:

1. Verses 1–4 (Cleansing of the leper)
2. Verses 5–13 (Healing the Centurion's servant)
3. Verses 14–17 (Healing of Peter's mother)
4. Verses 28–34 (Healing of Gergesene's demons)

The medicine was taken as prescribed by Doctor Jesus so that the healing process can begin. Without the biblical medicine taken in prescribed doses by Dr. Jesus, the healing process might be prolonged. With spiritual medicine, not only can people get healthy through salvation, grace, and mercy, but everyone around can become healthier.

Biblical medicine was prescribed by God through his son, Jesus Christ; thus, spiritual healing was coupled with spiritual living through the obedience to God's words and the teaching and preaching of Jesus Christ. The old creation is replaced by the crucifixion and resurrection of Jesus Christ, and this is the rule and guide of our future way of living.

The crucifying of afflicted infirmities will be removed from the recesses of the heart, and the spirit and be resurrected in the newness of Lord and Savior Jesus Christ. Let's first examine what God is saying to the world.

To aide with the healing process old thoughts must be removed to make room for biblical information. These thoughts impede growth and development and the acquisition of additional information. To be successful in acquiring current information, the purging of old information must take place. The difficulty arises when learned behavior must be relearned or de-educated in order to reeducate and break through the mind-sets.

The reeducation of the mind is fought fiercely because of established comfort zones. These comfort zones, although they are usable and contaminated with the neurosis of life experiences, can be removed. After close examination, we can explore strategies to assist with the reeducation process. Comfort zones must be neutralized or eradicated in order that the learner is ready for a change.

God uses affliction for the glorification of Himself. Humanity is given the opportunity to see the glory of God in action. In the story of Lazarus in the book of John, chapter 11:4, Jesus heard that Lazarus was sick and "he said that this sickness is not unto death, but for the glory of God, that the Son of God might be glorified thereby." God uses the same process in modern times for spiritual sickness to be healed in order to show His glory.

Many of the afflicted Christ-centered and faith-based people who worship in churches are living testimony of God's glory in their lives. The door of the medicine cabinet opened and biblical medicine is taken and the implementation of a new set of rule and regulations will begin.

Stewardship, defined in the simple form, is the management of God's people and God's resources. The people consist of all humanity and God's creations include the world and all of humanity as well as God himself. Resources are classified into several categories: housing, food, clothing, transportation, health, education, medical, budget, insurance, finance, money management, housekeeping, child-rearing or raising, household management, personal hygiene, cleanliness, fiscal management, buildings, and grounds.

This authorization is stated in the book of Genesis, chapter 1:28: "And let them have dominion, over the fish of the sea, and over the fowl of the air, and over everything that moves upon the face of the earth." God have given humanity the task to take care of all creations.

This is the beginning of the stewardship authority in order to ensure that the health and welfare of humanity is preserved and perpetuated for eternity. God loved his creations so much that He didn't want His creations to be eliminated under any circumstances.

Preservation of God's creations is the important task assigned to humanity. Genesis 1:27 states, "So God created man in His own image, in the image of God created him, male and female created them. And God blessed them, and God said unto them, be fruitful and multiply, and replenish the earth and subdue it."

The established rules and regulations in the Old Testament established a love affair between God and His creations in order to withstand the attacks of Satan. One of the main obligations of humanity is to ensure that the Word of God is taught in such a manner that it permanently produces the fruit of the spirit.

Galatians 5:22 states that "the fruit of the Spirit is love, joy, peace, longsuffering, gentleness, goodness, faith, meekness, temperance, against such there is no law."

Bible boot camp ensures that the word of God is administered differently than have been in past systems of education and information sharing. Conceptually, boot camp training once applied with military way of sharing information will remove the mysterious meaning from the Bible and use a different approach, through Christ-centered information sharing.

There will be no comments from the learner. Too often, learners want to share information about their relationship or personal experiences to demonstrate their so-called righteousness.

The session is not Bible study or Bible discussion but proper sharing of biblical information enables a listener the opportunity to evaluate the information and determine whether it is useful to him or her. When the collection of spiritual information applies to their situation of spiritual sickness, they will have additional options to exercise.

The learner is shown a different way to receive information by developing a reading style that applies to basic reading technology:

Step 1. The reader is requiring reading the Bible like it is a normal reading assignment.

Step 2. The learner is encouraged to read the Bible in the same manner that they would read fiction or nonfiction books. The learner with comprehension in mind should read slowly, chapter by chapter, to understand the storyline and the message from God. For example, the book of Matthew contains twenty-eight chapters. The learner is required to read all twenty-eight chapters slowly while enjoying the reading.

Step. 3. The reader will read the Bible sentence by sentence, paragraph by paragraph until they realize the working power of biblical information.

Familiarization of information is brought about by a step-by-step reading methodology proven to be successful having a rich history of longevity. Vietnam veterans said they were able to remember information from their boot camp experiences fifty or sixty years earlier indicating they were able to recite their first general orders and rifle number over and over daily.

Even today, many military veterans can remember their general orders and first rifle number because rote learning committed those things to memory. This methodology has proven successful in conquering new skills: driving, bicycle riding, swimming, and many other sports.

Dr. Richard Mayhue reports that "the details of daily living involve warfare against some enemies like Satan, circumstances, other people and even ourselves" (5). Mayhue said that this feeling of warfare encourages him to develop the Bible boot camp. His approach concentrates on normal church service not the transformation of the individual through military training. Our technology is designed to remove the cause of spiritual sickness and their symptoms.

After this sharing of spiritual information is applied, then the learner can begin to examine the incidents that has been blocking their blessings. The first step in spiritual healing is honesty to God. If the learner is not honest with God, then the learner cannot be honest with themselves or others.

Honesty has the power to open the door to life events that caused spiritual illness. The door opening is between the learner and God only.

When their personal experience humbles the learner, they become susceptible to the acquisition of new information, allowing the word of God to takeover and implement necessary changes. The mistake made is when they are not serving God but serving themselves or other people.

Matthew 4:8 states, "Again the devil taketh Him up unto an exceeding high mountain, and showeth Him all the kingdom of the world, and the glory of them. And said unto Him, all these things will I give thee, if thou will fall down and worship me."

The basis of this events demonstrates that Satan has the power to reward his followers but, under no circumstances, does he have the power or authority to bless anyone. It is believed that the most important role of the stewards of God is the carrying His word to his people. God's people have a survival mode that will enable them to resist the temptations of the world information systems.

The journey for spiritual healing starts to take place once spiritual sickness has been identified and the learner is ready to receive Godly information and seek God's Kingdom and His righteousness. Let the change begin after the removal of past spiritual sickness symptoms, named stressors, which lead to anger and produce disobedience.

Various stressors are discovered due to spiritual sickness. Stressors can be classified as physical stress, psychological stress, and cultural stress as discovered by a Bible study class at Mt. Pilgrim Baptist Church in Lugoff, South Carolina. The study group identified a small number of stressor classifications.

Physical Stressors—developed from the below list of infirmities:

- Death: the loss of a love one family or friend.
- Accidents: automobile driving or riding; job-related, hit by car, fighting, shooting, falling down; and non-job related, fire, poison, animal attack.
- Finance: living from paycheck to paycheck, not having savings or money for emergencies.
- Employment and unemployment: executive positions, CEO, president, vice president, upper management, executive supervisors.
- Jobs or jobless: maintenance and repair, technical, clerical, administration, construction workers, plumbers, electricians, iron workers, masons, carpenters, sheet rockers, labors.
- Underemployment: low wages, very low wages, living on tips, minimum wages.
- Bills: late payments, no payments, partial payment, high interest credit cards, living on credit cards, bad credit or no credit reports.
- Food: improper eating, fast food, improper nutritional, sugar, lard, uncooked, expired, contaminated, improper storage, rat and roach infestation, dirty preparation area.

- Housing: paying more than 30 percent of income, rent dodging, late rent payment, late mortgage payment, homelessness, over-housing, lease violations.
- Education: inferior, illiterate.
- Medical: amputation, accident, combat injuries, fights, shootings, missing limbs, blindness, hearing problems, cripple, wheelchair bound, deformed body, birth defects, heart problems, HIV/AIDS, cancer, diabetics, arthritis, high blood pressure, breathing illness, joint replacement.
- Mental illness: stigma, improper or no treatment, behavior.
- Criminal activities: illegal drug use and sale, prostitution, murder, robbery, carjacking, rape, kidnapping, purse snatching, car theft, stealing, bullying.
- Drug and alcohol abuse: treatment, counseling, detoxification centers, AAA.
- Aging process: elderly abuse, elderly housing, family support, discrimination, lack of respect, expensive medication and treatment.
- Transportation: car needs repair, no insurance, youth joyriding without permission, traffic violations, fines, court appearance, accident reports, insurance cost rising, unable to go to work.
- Communication: house phone, cell phones, lack of communication within a family, destroys family relationship, excessive time on the cell phone, cell phone used inappropriately at dinner, restaurants during family conversations.
- Weight: excessive weight impacts jobs, health, friendship, resentment from others, name-calling, unable to participate in outdoor activities, no exercise or playtime.
- Language: unable to understand domestic and foreign conversation, isolation from social activities, employment, limited job selection or type of available jobs.
- Poverty: daily living, housing, health, welfare, education, employment, hunger, clothing.

- Marriage: compatibility, finance, employment, religion, children, childless, family and friends, transportation, education.
- Divorce: devastation, family structure changed, loss of income, court, alimony, child support, infidelity, sexual change, homosexuality, child abuse, drugs, alcohol, battery.
- Pregnancy: morning sickness, medical problems developed during pregnancy, premature birth, miscarriages, breakups, not being married, depending on family for financial support.
- Breakups: guilty feeling, trying to figure out what went wrong, the blaming game, anger, hurt, pain, violence, guilt, why, can't we get back together?
- Caretaking: Can I get some help? I have no time for me, lack of family support, break time, health of the sick, feeding, cleaning patient and house, exhaustion, lack of sleep, stage of sickness, long term or short term, sorrowful, concerned about the rate and kind of care is needed and changes necessary.
- New neighborhood, new school, new friends.

Psychological Stress—traumatic events, lack of human love, isolation, withdrawal, society's rejection, discrimination, loneliness, friendship, sexual preference, language, obesity, poverty.

Cultural Stress—acceptance, citizenship, religious customs, racial purification, ethnic discrimination, clothing, language, marriage ceremony, idol worshipping, burial ceremony (cremation).

The learners realized that the majority of the manufactured stress makers have been hidden in their comfort zones and turned into coping skills. These stressors require a great amount of energy to contain them in a remote storage area of the brain. The stressors become part of one's history, and when the stress button is pushed, an instant reaction takes place equal to the original event.

Through a Bible boot camp biblical training method, learners will receive a closer and deeper analysis of stressors and their debilitating effects on scripture readings. The employed method will simplify the reading and understanding of scriptures. Each scripture has several catchwords that emphasize the message of the scripture:

- Jeremiah 26:13—hear and obey
- Matthew 6:33—seek and righteousness
- Matthew 16:24—deny and follow
- Matthew 11:28—come and rest
- John 8:31—word and disciple
- John 8:32—truth and free
- John15:3—clean and word

These catchwords are focused on scriptures with the remaining words as qualifiers or supporting words. The focus words provide clear understanding of biblical information, which leads to spiritual understanding and application.

The learners allow biblical information to impact the transformation and detoxify worldly information. The book of Matthew is where Godly learning begins. The Sermon on the Mount presents a set of scriptures outlining Christian virtues, which is a very important place to start on the journey of spiritual healing.

These scriptures not only instruct but examine the learner's awareness as to God's relationship and desire for his people. Examine some requirements that will cement the word of God through rehabilitation and transformation process.

Matthew 4:23–24 states, "And Jesus went about all Galilee, teaching in their synagogues, and preaching the Gospel of the Kingdom, and healing all manner of sickness and all manner of disease among the people. And his fame went throughout all Syria and they brought unto him all sick people that were taken with divers disease and torments, and those which was possessed with devils and those which were lunatic and those that had the palsy and he healed them."

That same Jesus who provided miracles and medical assistance is still working today. Healing God's people is part of His mission to bring sinners to repentance. Without the message from God the

Father through His Son, Jesus Christ, salvation is not possible. The Bible states that Jesus didn't come for the righteous but for the sinners to repent. Sin comes from spiritual sickness, which is disobedience to God's word.

Jesus as healer and doctor is demonstrated in other verses, such as in Matthew 8:2–3: "And behold there came a leper and, Him, saying, Lord if thou wilt, thought canst make me clean. And Jesus put forth His hand, and touch him saying, I will; be thou clean. And immediately his leprosy was cleaned."

Matthew 8:13—Centurion servant healed
Matthew 8:15—Healing Peter's mother in law
Matthew 8:32—Casting out devils

The book of Jeremiah, chapter 26:13 states, "Therefore now amend your ways and your doing and obey the voice of the Lord your God; and the Lord will repent him of the evil that he hath pronounced against you."

Here, God, when calling your name, is telling you to perform an activity. After hearing His voice, God states that His people must learn how to obey. Afterward, He will remove the curse he has pronounced unto His people, which demonstrated their spiritual sickness through their disobedient behavior.

As a form of communication, God uses our spiritual and physical sickness to glorify Himself as he shows His power and authority. God's glory is shown in several places in the Bible. In the book of John, chapter 11:4, it says, "This sickness is not unto death, but for the glory of God, that the Son of God might be glorified thereby." The glory of God has been shown many times in life, but because of spirital sickness, it was very difficult to recognize the glory of God.

Eliminating useless information helps enlighten God's presence by providing acquisition of accurate biblical information providing spiritual healing. The type of Bible selected is important for the Word of God to simplify the correct translation aiding new learners. The New International Version (NIV) is the recommended translation of the King James Version (KJV) that many congregations suggest.

Reading a complete chapter at different speed and focus are steps that will aid a new learner. The first reading is for the familiarity of the chapter. The next reading is read slowly for a better understanding. The third reading, sentence by sentence, helps the identification of words and helps determine the depth and real meaning of the sentence. The additional words give support to the bottom line.

This reading method is stated again because of the importance that the new learners in the Bible not be intimidated by the form of literature.

Another form of receiving God's words is by listening to the Bible. The talking Bible becomes a unique means of developing a personal relationship with God. Listening to the Bible removes personal interpretation. This method of spiritual information can be taken in several ways. Listen to the talking Bible during long-distance driving, to and from work or other destinations. Listen to the Bible while shopping at stores, exercising, or around the house during other activities, and even while watching television when the sound of the TV is in the mute mode.

Praying about daily issues and concerns helps one develop a personal relationship with Him and this simple approach makes it easier to be honest and open and develop a close relationship with God. This personal relationship establishes a personal communication schedule and enhances the learner's ability to get to know God through reading and hearing his words.

According to the scripture, learners can communicate with God through prayer, dance, praise, worship, singing, and songs. There are 128 scriptures on prayer. Praise is mentioned 259 times and worship is stated 158 times.

Prayer: KJV—128, NIV—154
Dance: KJV–19, NIV—13
Sing: KJV—169, NIV—158
Praise: KJV—259, NIV—363
Worship: KJV—188, NIV—254
Song: KJV—61, NIV—110

There appears to be no limit for learners communicating with God because of diverse personalities and spiritual sickness. It appears that the worshippers of antiquity used more praise and worship scriptures when communicating with God. The choices are available as shown in the chart above.

Nonverbal communication with God is very powerful and doesn't require speaking to people who may not want to be bothered. Demonstrate the power of the word of God enough to wear caps and clothing that articulate the Christ center of the personal relationship with God through nonverbal communication.

Nonverbal communication can encourage the wearer to develop a stronger relationship with God by demonstrating that they are not ashamed of the Gospel of Jesus Christ. Be a soldier for God's army. A young man stated that we might be the only Bible that people will ever read.

God's spirit informs the learner that silent prayer maybe the most honest and sincere method of communication because it comes from one's heart and directed straight to Him.

This form of prayer and communication is honest, straightforward without any mental reservation or equivocation. God, and God alone, hears and receives silent prayers that are fervent and righteous. The book of Matthew 6:6 states, "But thou, when thou prayest, enter into thy closet, and when thou hast shut thy door, pray to thy Father which is in secret, and thy Father which seeth in secret shall reward thee openly."

This verse states that silent prayer is for God only; therefore, the learner is not seeking acknowledgement from humanity but reward from God. The constant communication with God, the creator of the heaven and earth, can't be over emphasized.

Gospel music resonates in my mind because of the continued playing and hearing of God's messages through music. Constant repeating and hearing allow Godly information to assist in spiritual healing.

It is very important that a learner realizes and understands the importance of other means of communing with God other that prayer. Prayer has been emphasized over the life of modern worship services, but present-day focus is praise and worship where all members of the congregation participate.

Prayer has been a very important part of worship services, but the true picture of prayer does not receive enough attention. The book of James, chapter 5:16 states, "Confess your faults one to another, and pray one for another, that ye may healed. The effectual fervent prayer of a righteous man availeth much."

Two words, fervent and righteousness, are the two most significant words in this sentence, which brings prayer to another circumstance. Righteousness comes from obedience to the word of God, which determines whether God will respond to your prayer. The following are scriptures that demonstrate when God does not response to prayer:

- Proverbs 1:28: "Then shall they call upon me, but I will not answer; they shall seek me early, but they shall not find me."
- Psalm 18:41: "They cried, but there was none to save them; even unto the Lord, but He answered them not."
- Psalm 66:18: "If I regard iniquity in my heart the Lord will not hear me."
- Isaiah 1:15: "And when ye spread forth your hands, I will hide my eyes from you; yea when ye make many prayers, I will not hear: your hands are full of blood."
- Jeremiah 11:11: "Therefore thus saith the Lord, Behold I will bring evil upon them, which they will not be able to escape; and though they cry unto me, I will not hearken unto them."
- Jeremiah 14:12: "When they fast, I will not hear their cry; and when they offer burnt offering and oblation, I will not accept them, but I will consume them by the sword, and by the famine, by the pestilence."
- Ezekiel 8:18: "Therefore will I also deal in fury, mine eye shall not spare, neither will I have pity; and though they cry in my ears with a loud voice, yet I will not hear them."

- Zachariah 7:13: "Therefore it will come to pass, that as he cried, and they would not hear; so, they cried, and I would not hear, said the Lord of hosts."
- Micah 3:4: "Then shall they cry unto the Lord, but he will not hear them: he will even hide His face from them at that time, as they have behaved themselves ill in their doings."
- John 9:31 "Now we know that God hearth not sinners. But if any man be a worshipper of God, and doeth his will him he hearth."
- James 4:3: "Ye ask, and receive not, because ye ask amiss, that ye may consume it upon your lusts."

These scriptures are not preached because prayer has been misused and so long as that minister, as well as church members, believes that God answer all prayers. To share these scriptures with learners will encourage them to be righteous through Godly information. God can only be worshipped in His spirit and His truth, which are the true scriptural word of God.

Not sharing the Godly truth is just as bad as committing sin. Too often, scripture are modified, taken out of context and content in order to prove a point which is not Bible based. This is as sinful as taking Christ out of Christmas by undermining the sovereignty of God. Without biblical information, hypocritical life prevails.

Matthew 5:18 states, "For verily I say unto you, Till heaven and earth pass, one jot or one tittle shall in no wise pass from the law till all be fulfilled. Whosoever therefore shall break one of these least commandments, and shall teach men so, he shall be called the least in the kingdom of heaven; but whosoever do and teach them, the same shall be called great in the kingdom of heaven." When the messenger shares the incorrect interpretation of Godly information, they are accountable to God for their actions. The Bible says that no liar will enter the kingdom of heaven. It's very important that the word of God be shared correctly.

The Bible states in Romans 12:1, "I beseech ye therefore brethen, by the mercies of God, that ye present your bodies a living sacrifice, holy, acceeptable unto God, which is your reasonable services. And be not conformeed to this world: but be ye transformed by the renewimg of your mind, that ye may prove what is that good, and acceptable, and perfect, will of God."

Since the body is the temple of God, it is important that learners accept and realize that each person has a responsibility to keep God's temple spiritualy clean, which can only be performed through God's scriptures. The living sacrifice is when the enemy of God tempts learners to perform ungodly behavior; the learners' spirit of discernment prevent them from sinning.

Exodus 20:3 states, "Thou shall have no other gods before me." The word "god" pertains to any activities that would interfer or distract humanity, from having God first in their lives. The gods that are mentioned are people, jobs, money, fame, fortune, titles in church, cars, gold, jewery, and any other material items.

God's desire for humanity to experience holiness and righteousness through obedience to Godly information, which is the Bible. The Bible states that if you love God and obey His rules and regulations, it would be difficult to serve two masters. Matthew 6:24 "No man can serve two masaters: Ye cannot serve God and mammon."

Dr. John Sutherland Bonnell states that "our greatest need at this time is to bring the healing power of God to bear upon countless thousand of persons who are overborne by the burden and problems of life" (6). Bonnell said that it essential that people go back to the commision that Jesus gave his apostles, which was to heal the sick and preach the gospel.

Matthew 10:1 states, "And when He called unto Him his twelve disciples, He gave them power against unclean spirits, to cast them out, and to heal all manner of sickness and all manner of disease." Spiritual healing increases as Godly information is shared, received, understood and applied. This scripture validates Bonnell's words about Christians going back to the initial purpose of evangalism.

Spiritual healing has been employed on physical healing since the beginning of time. Science believed that the soul of humanity enforced by faith has performed miracles that medical doctors cannot explain. Dr. Henry E. Margineau states that "every event discovered by the best accredited sciencetist show the the universe is friendly to spiritual forces." Dr. William G. Pollard writes "that it is incoceiveable that the entire material universe of which we are aware may one day be dissolved, leaving only nonmaterial reality" (42).

Second Corinthian 5:17 states, "Therefore if any man be in Christ, he is a new creature: old things are passed away; behold, all things are become new. And all things are of God, who hath reconciled us to himself by Jesus Christ, and hath given us the ministry of reconciliation."

In these scripture, God is speaking through Apostle Paul. He says that when people accept Jesus Christ as their Lord and Savior, they become a new person, born in the Godly spirit and their behavior is changed. Holiness and righteousness become the byproduct of their behavior, and change has taken place.

Through reconciliation with God, all sins are washed away, and God has forgiven past trangressions for those who really believe in their hearts that Jesus Christ is the son of God. Spiritual healing through reconciliation will encourage true believers to seek God's kingdom and righteousness and prioritize their life through the teachings of Jesus Christ in the Holy Words of God.

After reading the book, *The God-Centered Life*, by Josh Moody, I became energized by my mission to providing information to people in order to help them come to a decision about their lives, which is to accept Jesus Christ as their Lord and Savior. This diffuicult task has been contaminated by dishonest methods of suppling Godly information to spiritually sick people.

I apologize to God for being led astray by the human desires to satisfy themselves instead of glorifying Him. Thank God for assignig this mission of grief education. Past grief, fear and anger must be rooted out via spiritual healing in order to eliminate spiritual sickness. "I once was lost but now I am found, was blind but now I see." Thank God and the teachings of Jesus Christ and his Christian drill instruction to get back on the mission that was ascribed by God almighty.

The twelve disciples were the first group of drill instructors Jesus trained and dispatched unto the world to heal and teach the spiritually sick and infirmed people.

Matthew 10: 1–8 states:

> And when he had called unto him his twelve disciples, he gave them power against unclean spirits, to cast them out, and to heal all manner of sickness and all manner of disease. Now the names of the twelve apostles are these; The first, Simon, who is called Peter, and Andrew his brother; James the son of Zebedee, and John his brother; Philip, and Bartholomew; Thomas, and Matthew the publican; James the son of Alphaeus, and Lebbaeus, whose surname was Thaddaeus; Simon the Canaanite, and Judas Iscariot, who also betrayed him. These twelve Jesus sent forth, and commanded them, saying, Go not into the way of the Gentiles, and into any city of the Samaritans enter ye not: But go rather to the lost sheep of the house of Israel. And as ye go, preach, saying, The kingdom of heaven is at hand. Heal the sick, cleanse the lepers, raise the dead, cast out devils: freely ye have received, freely give.

On the highway to heaven, like any road trips, there will be obstacles along the journey. If one was traveling from Columbis, South Carolina, to Atlanta, Georgia, one would encounter traffic slowdown and many times will come to a complete stop due to road hazards, brokendown vehicles, car wrecks, large truck slowing down traffic, police lights shining, tow trucks, ambulance, red and blue lights with sirens blaring excessive noise, and other distractions but the trip continues.

Potholes are encountered and detours may have to be taken, but the goal is to reach Atlanta safe and sound. Sometimes, one needs to stop for gas or use the restrooms, but the journey must go on. Finally, with relief in sight, the destination, Atlanta, is reached and living accommodations are available but the journey is not over.

Often necessary are rest and relaxation following a long road trip because of exhaustive driving and hazardous road experiences.

But even with navigational assistance, the mission may not be accomplished until at the destination.

Although the navigator was constantly being utilized, preoccupation and conversation defeated the assistance. The navigator was taken for granted, but faith in the navigator proved successful. How would the journey turn out if there was no navigator? How many times would the driver of the vehicle be lost in an unfamiliar city? To avoid being lost in a strange city or area, chances are the driver would have to seek direction from several sources and still be lost.

The highway to Heaven is no different, even with pastors, teachers, ministers, evangelists, and other instructors of the Gospel of Jesus Christ. Amazing Grace, an old-time hymn instructs on embarking on a journey to a heavenly destination with the words, "I once was lost, but now I am found." No matter how many hours are spent in research and Bible study, many obstacles get in the way of the journey on the highway to heaven. Spiritual sickness is real, alive, and operating twenty-four hours a day. Even the Christ-centered or faith-based life includes obstacles and accidents on the heavenly trip.

The profile of a passenger on the heavenly journey recognizes that God is the ticket holder, and Jesus Christ arranged the travel itinerary; the conductor is important to view passengers who have the desire to attend and their different reasons.

The church is the place for purchasing tickets and boarding place before the heavenly journey begins.

The passengers consist of members from every social and economical strata that exist. These diverse population is in conflict with each other, and each strive for key name recognition and preferred seating.

Their desire for a ticket upgrade is not available. Ticket upgrades and special fares only take place prior to the journey. Seeking first-class seating while paying for coach is not possible.

This is the same behavior that exists in the church where new members are seeking leadership position. Although they are not qualified to hold these offices, but they demand and command these offices in a unrighteous manner. Their desire is not to serve God but to gain power and authority over God's people.

These offices must not be executed from a world information system. Many applicants will bring abusive behavior to their work assignments and project their hostile feelings unto church activities. They are not aware of the spiritual sickness and sublimate their hostility. A desire to ventilate their feelings in a Christ-centered environment is devastating to the congregation.

The necessity to grow in biblical knowledge and information may not be their desire because of spiritual sickness. Spiritual sickness not only impedes their ability to serve God in spirit and truth but may also have adverse effects in the healing process. These are the people that the Bible boot camp training can really help. Same people.

Church attendance varies amongst people. Some attend to boost their resume and socialization instead of for fellowship. Others attend because they are in trouble due to their criminal behavior and want to impress the court system when they face the judge, thinking they will gain a better verdict if found guilty of a criminal offense, whether it is small or large, misdemeanor or a felony.

There are honest people who come to the realization that life has not been kind and seek God's kingdom and righteousness. These people know that God is the answer to their prayers and surrender to Christian teachings and doctrine.

According to ministerial emphasis on dressing properly for church attendance, it depends upon the attendee's type of work and their working hours resulting in working people who dress up for services and events. Some dress to demonstrate fashion or a search for a companion and are not wearing clothing for the glory of God.

The church is like a hospital, where the patients consist of drug addicts, alcoholics, homosexuals, bullies, prostitutes, the mentally ill, pimps, hustlers, womanizers, sexual perverts, promiscuity, STD carriers and more. With all of this going on, physical and verbal fighting, stealing, child sex abuse and more, spiritual healing must be approached differently.

These patients must be received with great amount of Godly love and understanding. They do not need to be reminded of their infirmities but respected as children of the most high God. These "patients" need to hear that they were made in the image of God and God's love for them will never change but they must be born again.

To assist with the preparation for the journey to heaven, every need must be considered and taken into consideration. Godly information from the Bible must be shared with the passenger, and they must agree to the conditions. Thus, a personal valid contract with God must be executed and obeyed. If the contract is broken, God will forgive and provide a new contract.

The heavenly journey will experience many obstacles, trials, and tribulations; the difference is that the navigator for this journey will be conducted by Jesus Christ. Philippians 4:13 states, "I can do all things through Christ which strengtheneth me." Since Jesus is the conductor and navigator, the heavenly journey can be successful.

Ozell Dunlap states, "Life is a journey that some of us started on a long time ago, and some not so long ago. A journey that will one day lead us to a place where will be fulfilled, set free, and made whole. A place where we will find all the things, we have searched for all our lives."

She states that "The journey one travel day by day, the difficulties, detours and all other encounters we face along the way" (19).

Life's journey is not complete until the end times, when Jesus shall return to judge His Father's creations. Matthew 24:3–14 states:

> And as he sat upon the mount of Olives, the disciples came unto him privately, saying, tell us, when shall these things be? and what shall be the sign of thy coming, and of the end of the world? And Jesus answered and said unto them, Take heed that no man deceive you. For many shall come in my name, saying, I am Christ; and shall deceive many. And ye shall hear of wars and rumors of wars: see that ye be not troubled: for all these things must come to pass, but the end is not yet. For nation shall rise against nation, and kingdom against kingdom: and there shall be famines, and pestilences, and earthquakes, in divers places. All

these are the beginning of sorrows. Then shall they deliver you up to be afflicted, and shall kill you: and ye shall be hated of all nations for my name's sake. And then shall many be offended, and shall betray one another, and shall hate one another. And many false prophets shall rise, and shall deceive many. And because iniquity shall abound, the love of many shall wax cold. But he that shall endure unto the end, the same shall be saved. And this gospel of the kingdom shall be preached in all the world for a witness unto all nations; and then shall the end come.

The end of the journey may or may not be completed if passengers lose their boarding passes. Without Godly preparation through biblical information to transform worldly information into Christian behavior, the trip is delayed. Preparation time is needed for the cleaning power of God's word to become effective. John15:3 states, "Now ye are clean through the word which I have spoken unto you."

In Bible boot camp, God is the speaker and presenter of His own Word. The presenter or instructor directs the learners to use the Bible as the rule and guide on their earthy journey, directing them to listen to the audible Bible repeatedly until they receive understanding. According to Gordon D. Fee and Douglas Stuart, the Bible is "that is we believe that God's Word for us today is first of all precisely what the Word was for previous generations. Thus, we have two tasks: first to find out the text originally meant, secondarily we must learn to hear the same meaning in the variety of new or different contexts of our own day" (11).

Bible boot camp encourages learners to develop a greater understanding and adherence to Godly information. Repeatedly reading, listening, and understanding the teachings of the Bible will prepare one for the heavenly boarding pass.

Once on the heavenly journey, the need for constant infusion of biblical information, training, and application must be satisfied.

Godly information cannot be exhibited unless behavioral modification is shown through interactions with family, friends, and strangers.

Matthew 10:34 states, "Think not that I come to send peace on earth; I came not to send peace, but a sword. For I came to set a man at variance against his father, and the daughter against her mother, and the daughter in law against her mother in law. And a man's foes shall be they of his own household."

These scriptures confirm and support worldly concerns that connotes spiritual ideology and Godly support and understanding. Without faith, it is impossible to please God. A man writes these words of encouragement. These writings are from a phantom writer: "As life journey is exposed and brought to light, the present state of humanity is the sum total of errors and omissions. Past gone days are just that but we can and feel where we came from by looking where we are at. Exam who you are and see the manifestation of your growth, value, and worth to humanity."

Humanity needs a helping hand to continue the empowerment God assigned us in the beginning of His creations. God needs our help. By being obedient to the will of God, humanity lends a helping hand to continue the empowerment God assigned to us in the beginning and we can excel, be fruitful, and multiply by remaining obedient.

Can you see with your mind where you came from and in what direction you are traveling? To heaven or hell! What is your destination and are you prepared and dressed for the trip? God cries out for humanity to be saved regardless of color, creed, nationality, ethnicity, political affiliation, or religious persuasion. Jesus said that He came so that the whole world might be saved.

As Jesus was having dinner with His disciples after healing the sick, the people cheered for Him and was amazed at his healing power. The scribes, Pharisees, and publicans began to question Jesus's authority and why He was eating with everyday people called sinners. Jesus states in Matthew 9:13, "I am not come to call the righteous but sinners to repentance." Who is your father and master?

After examining and identifying the causes of spiritual sickness, a treatment plan must be developed and implemented to remove the causes, and the symptoms should disappear. This initial focus of instruction is Jeremiah 26:13: "Therefore now amend your ways and your doing, and obey the voice of the Lord your God; and the Lord will repent him of the evil that he hath pronounced against you."

The call for the desire to change the way humanity is living a life based on world information instead of Godly information is vital. God is displeased with the behavior of humanity and pronounced a curse. World information system develops spiritual sickness, the result of unrighteousness and the desire to satisfy fleshly needs. Jeremiah is calling for humanity's behavior to be modified so that God will remove the curse that He has ordered.

Obeying the voice of the Lord is very important because, many times, people listen but do not hear because of the distractions that is taking place around them is more important in their lives. The preoccupation with issues that interferes with the solicitation of approval from family, friends, and others overrides the voice of God calling their name.

God is saying, "Listen and obey my scriptures. Your behavior will change, and I will remove the evil I have pronounced against you." In order for humanity to hear and obey God's instructions, they must have a desire for a Christ-centered life. This desire may be motivated by many different circumstances, which has invaded their comfort zones. Nevertheless, they will be seeking a change in their lives.

Once humanity hears the voice of God calling their name, they will have a different focus of reality. Matthew 6:33 states, "But seek ye first the kingdom of God, and his righteousness; and all these things shall be added unto you." The most important part of this scripture is the seeking of God. Emphasizing the word "first," gives complete power to trust God in the deliverance and fulfillment of His authority. God is a rewarder of those that seek Him, as stated in Hebrew 11:6, "But without faith it is impossible to please Him: for he that cometh to God must believe that He is, and that He is a rewarder of them that diligently seek Him."

The next word that need to be emphasized is the word" righteousness," which can only come from God through obedience of His word. According to the dictionary, "righteousness is the quality of being morally correct and justifiable. Considered as attribute that implies that a person's actions are justified and can have the connotation that the person has been judged as leading a life that is pleasing to God."

Dr. Thomas A Harris states that "transactional analysis had given rise to the concept of adult, parent, and child developed personality" (18). Understanding transactional analysis assists in Bible boot camp learning method and this methodology is productive for changing and identifying the psychological personality through conversations. The conversation, once identified, determines what personality is being used and will assist in addressing spiritual sickness.

Berne states that "as you watch and listen to people you can see them change before your eyes. It is a total kind of change. There are simultaneous changes in facial expressions, vocabulary, gestures, posture, and body functions, which may cause the face to flush, the heart to pound, or the breathing becoming rapid" (18).

Physical reaction is important when Godly information is being shared with learners. When observing the learner's behavior, a determination is made by the instructor as to the impact made due to the acquisition of Godly information.

In the book of Matthew, chapter 10:36, it says, "And a man's foes shall be they of his own household." The writings of Thomas appear to be aligned with Thomas's parent and family and the inability to establish communication with each other due to spiritual sickness.

Cross talking happens because of a developed mind-set that established comfort zones to defend from pain. These defensive states are the results of fear from perceived invasion or condemnation of established comfort zones.

The continuation of Jesus's sermon in Matthew 10:34 states, "Think not that I am come to send peace on earth: I came not to send peace but a sword." This is an emergency alert and warning to the people of God. The sword is the word of God that compels humanity to be obedient to the scriptures or perish from spiritual sickness to eventual spiritual death. This warning provides sinners with the opportunity to repent.

Jesus continues to preach and confront humanity in Matthew 10:35: "For I am come to set a man at variance against his father, and the daughter against her mother, and the daughter in law against her mother in law." The central theme of Harris's writing is the analysis of family interactions.

Dr. Eric Berne states that Harris's concept can be considered from a game perspective where "an ongoing series of complementary ulterior transactions progressing to a well-defined, predictable outcome" (54). The game concept provides several options, first is to play the game according to the rules of the game presented to you. The second option is to play the game and change the rules. The third option is to reject the game and not play. The fourth option is playing the game according to the verses in the Bible. What does the Bible say? How would Jesus play and respond to the game?

Since righteousness comes from God, learners should be aware that the accumulation of Godly information should be the immediate objective. Spiritual sickness identified, spiritual healing has begun, the march to full recovery is possible.

John 3:16 states, "For God so loved the world, that he gave his only begotten Son, that whosoever believeth in him should not perish, but have everlasting life."

Matthew 11:28 states, "Come unto me, all ye that labor and are heavy laden, and I will give you rest. Take my yoke upon you, and learn of me; for I am meek and lowly in heart; and ye shall find rest upon your souls. For my yoke is easy, and my burden is light."

Since Jesus is the door to eternal salvation, learners must be convinced that He is the Son of God with all power at His disposal. The convincing can only come from reading, listening, understanding, and believing the words of God written in the Bible.

"Come unto me" requires Bible boot camp learners to have a desire for fellowship with God through the teaching of Jesus Christ. The door of opportunity is available, but Jesus will not take away the free choice that God provided since the beginning of creation. Godly love is so strong that the entry into God's kingdom must be executed by willing participants.

The invitation to righteousness has to be accepted by those learners that feel that spiritual healing is in the word of God through Jesus Christ who died for all sinners. The scripture has identified infirmities in our lives and is providing an opportunity for rehabilitation, rejuvenation, and restoration.

Bible boot camp requires learners to rely on their motivation to acquire biblical knowledge due to their focus and aspirations to obtain a better relationship with God. This can happen if the expectation of righteousness is their goal.

Productive study habits must be coupled with time management. Designated and setting aside time for the Bible assists and develops a study plan predicated on the boot camp methodology. Repeating and repeating equates to drill, drill until the Godly information becomes automatic and comes forth without thinking about a Godly response.

The Godly response to worldly inquiries will allow the continuation of growth and development toward a Christ-centered living.

Initially, mistakes will be made, but due to perseverance and the quest for graduation, the constant drills will eliminate all mistake. Perfect Godly practice, patience, time, and repetition will overcome all obstacles. And impediments will not prevail.

Matthew 16:24 states, "If any man will come after me, let him deny himself, and take up his cross, and follow me." Jesus is saying the step in being a disciple is to deny one's self. Self-denial is when one's faith in God is so strong that, no matter what sacrifice is required to obtain self-denial, it is imperative that the learners accept the challenge.

Romans 12:1 states, "I beseech you therefore, brethren, by the mercies of God, that ye present your bodies a living sacrifice, holy acceptable to God, which is your reasonable service. Be not conformed to this world, but be ye transformed by renewing of your mind, that ye may prove what is that good, and acceptable and perfect, will of God."

What an awesome task must be undertaken to prove that one is ready to be a soldier of God's army. To understand that, trials and tribulations will surface and challenge your desire to be successful in God's army. Personal weakness will be brought to light, and defeat upon defeat will have one questioning their choice to follow the teachings of Jesus Christ.

Bible boot camp prepares learners to be followers as well as leaders. It has been proven by military conquest that if you are not a good follower, you cannot be a leader. Leaders are required to obey orders and accomplish the mission at all cost. Military training is to kill or be killed, but try to stay alive for another engagement with the enemy.

The enemy is the devil, and Jesus is preparing His troops to go into world to save His followers. The soldiers of Jesus are not to carry any food, clothing, or money. Matthew 10:6 states, "Go to the lost sheep of the house of Israel. As ye go preach, saying, the kingdom of heaven is at hand. Heal the sick, cleanse the lepers, raise the dead, cast out devils, freely ye have received, freely give."

These same instructions from Jesus is applicable today as it was in previous years. Spiritual survival is very important to God in order to save His spiritually sick followers from spiritual death.

Spiritual sickness is revealed when the only tools in a friendly environment is the Word of God. Weakness exposed, friends disappears, music doesn't sound the same, and loneliness is you only companion. The realization that a metamorphosis is taking place, confusion sets in, and the glory of God is calling for perseverance. You're in God's army. Bible boot camp is your new duty station.

John 8:31 states, "If ye continue in my word, then are you my disciple indeed, and ye shall know the truth shall set you free." Bible boot camp emphasizes the use of the Bible as your total source of information to resolve all issues and concerns that causes spiritual sickness. Jesus is saying that, in order for spiritual sickness to be treated, the healing must come from the Lord of God.

The word of God comes when the learner agrees to becoming a disciple of Jesus Christ. Being a student of the Bible qualifies a learner to biblical discipleship for additional biblical training.

Bible boot camp demands and commands total obedience to the word of God, allowing the medicine in the Bible to taken and to begin the healing process.

Present your bodies as living sacrifices wholly accepted by God as your reasonable services. The body is the temple of God that houses God's holy spirit. God requires a clean temple, and the cleansing can only come from the word of God. Godly information, when adhered to, is so powerful that the increased faith in God will satisfy all issues and concerns and will help you on your journey toward spiritual healing.

In the book of Philippians, chapter 4:13, it states, "I can do all things through Christ which strengthened me." God's army is marching to Zion, carrying the blood-stained banner against the enemy of God. We must realize that this spiritual battle is not ours but the God almighty. The richness of scriptures cannot be prepared by any other readings. Jesus guarantees that if you obey Him, all your desires and expectations will granted.

In the book of 2 Corinthian, chapter 5:17, it states, "Therefore, if any man be in Christ, he is a new creature: old things are passed away; behold, all things become new." As Jesus died and rose again, humanity needs to experience spiritual death in order for new birth to prevail. Being born again is not a physical event but a spiritual activity that produces a new outlook on life through the word of God.

Being born again allows Godly training to produce the fruit of the spirit, which consists of love, joy, peace, long-suffering, gentleness, goodness, faith, meekness, and temperance as stated in the book of Galatians, chapter 5:22 and 23. Any indication of these virtues demonstrates that the Bible boot camp is assisting in spiritual healing from the hard work and time spent in the words of God. Godly information is strengthened through constant hard work, drilling, and obedience to the learned scriptures.

To emphasize the love that will come with being born again is stated in John 15:7: "If ye abide in me and my words abide in you, ye shall ask what ye will, and it shall be done unto you." Jesus is saying that God will be glorified in the fruit that disciples and learners bring to kingdom building. John 15:9, 11, 12: "As the Father hath loved me, so have I loved you, continue ye in my love… This is my commandment, that you love one another as I have loved you. These things have I spoken to you that my joy remain in you, and your joy might be full." The fruit of the spirit play an important role in the transformation process.

Leaving the world is not an easy task, but it must be done in order that the desired results are exhibited through the transformation process. It is important the learners attending the Bible Boot Camp to spend a small amount of time writing and sharing their experience.

The question was how has the Bible boot camp impacted your life? The responses varied according to the length of time that the learners have been in training:

- Learner 1: Yes! I have really learned a lot about how to do things the right way and understand how to put it together in words. Learning God's words and what he is saying to me means a lot. His words are everything to me because I use His words for my kids and grandkids. This class have really helped me a lot.
- Learner 2: It has helped me to see things in a more open way and to read and understand the word more in my daily life and the way I treat others.
- Learner 3: Bible boot camp has impacted my life by making better choices and controlling my thoughts while going through life. It also helps me to pass the message on to others that doesn't know anything about word of God.
- Learner 4: Bible boot camp impacted my life and my daily life. It makes me feel the same way Peter felt when he betrayed Jesus. When he betrayed him three times, when he had always said that he will never betray him, He said he would die first. Now I am better in all my ways.
- Learner 5: It has impacted my life, knowing that I'm not alone in my healing process. It has also confirmed what God has directly put into my heart about forgiving myself and others.
- Learner 6: Wow! What can I say about this awesome Bible boot camp? Bible boot camp has impacted both my personal and spiritual life for the better. I have been challenged to develop a personal and unique relationship with God almighty. I have been challenged to read the Bible daily and focus on Matthew, chapters 5, 6, and 7. I know now that it is the word God, and only the word of God that cleanse

me. I must talk to God about what grieves me in my life. The Bible has all the answers that I need.

- I should only speak for myself and not others. I must listen to God. God will speak to me. I have learned that I am sick. I have spiritual sickness that only the word of God can heal me from. Church is a hospital and it has what I need, but I must do self-examination. Seek God and His righteousness and all things will be added to me. I am to ask God to help me identify my grief in my life. I deal with stress on a daily basis. The word of God is a healer.
- Learner 7: Help me to understand order. Only at the time when needed; talk to my spirit. Better understand what grief really is. Help me to fix my mind-set. Better spiritual problems solved. Importance of the book of Matthew, chapters 5, 6, and 7.

John 14:12 states, "Verily, verily, I say unto you, he that believeth on me, the works that I do shall he do also; and greater works than these shall he do, because I go unto my father."

Jesus is saying that because of the required transformation from world information to Godly information; it is a process that learners must grow through. He is available to help. The disciples of Jesus had special times when the focus was to strengthen their faith in order that they would be encouraged to stay on their assignment of healing and preaching. Faith in God is very important if learners are to achieve their goals.

Hebrew 11:1 states, "Now faith is the substance of things hoped for, the evidence of things not seen." Faith takes the believer forward. Believing in an unseen God but still knowing that He will take care of all our earthly and spiritual needs is true faith. Faith is mentioned 336 times in KJV and 458 times in NIV translations. There are many scriptures that comes to mind, but the faith of a mustard seed will move problems out of one's life. The faith that not only heals your body but also heals your spirit. In Matthew, chapter 6, verses 8 and 32, God said, "I know what you need before you ask me, the problem comes when people do not experience the new birth." The new birth represents being born again and indicating that one is obedient to Godly information.

Faith in God is what humanity needs to be born again. He will make certain what needs are required to represent Godly information that logistical support will come together with the mission assigned by God.

When the flesh and worldly information interfere with the mission, which is spreading the Gospel of Jesus Christ, God will make your mission of righteousness successful because He's guiding the holy mission. First John 2:5 states, "Love not the world, neither the things that are in the world. If any man loves the world, the love of the Father is not in him. For all that is in the world, the lust of the flesh, and the lust of the eyes, and the pride of life, is not of the Father, but is of the world."

The world is the devil's domain; after he was cast down from heaven with one third of the angels, he is roaming the world to find who he can destroy.

The world needs to understand that Satan rewards his followers who bow down and worship him. In Matthew 4:8, the devil said to Jesus to look at the world, "The devil taketh Him up into an exceedingly high mountain, and sheweth Him all the kingdom of the world and the glory of them."

In the sane manner the devil tried to tempt Jesus, he will continue to try to tempt humanity by constantly pressuring them until they are broken down and sin rises its ugly head as spiritual sickness.

The breakdown is tempting because of vicious lies that the devil uses in order to let it manifest itself in contrast to the obedience to Godly information. The trap is sprung in verse 9 of Matthew 4, when the devil said, "All these things will I give thee, if thou wilt fall down and worship me." Spiritual sickness from world information provides direct access to the rewards from bowing down to the devil.

The corruption of God's follower is the warfare between the devil and God.

First Corinthian 10:13 states, "There hath no temptation taken you but such as is common to man, but God is faithful, who will not suffer you to be tempted above that you are able; but with the temptation also make a way to escape, that you may be able to bear it."

God is saying that when you are tempted by the devil, don't be concerned about the incident because the Holy Ghost will rescue you., provided you are seeking His kingdom and righteousness.

The Bible boot camp education system is based on the word of God that is written in scripture, understood, and applied. The proper allocation of time coupled with biblical study habits will provide success to adhere to this military type of training. Without biblical preparation, there can be no biblical application. The faith in God's ability to deliver one from harm's way is paramount to believing Godly information.

According to recent observation, I am encouraged that the transformation from a worldly information system to a Godly information system is possible given enough time., patience, and perseverance.

The learners must believe that the followers and imitators of Jesus Christ are special people.

First Peter 2:9 states, "But ye are a chosen generation, a royal priesthood, a holy nation, a peculiar people, that ye should shew forth the praises of him who has called you out of darkness into his marvelous light." To be chosen by God to minister to His people is an honor and should not be taken lightly.

Bible boot camp has fulfilled the desire of God by preparing followers that will carry His Godly words to all people. It is important that salvation through the administration of grace be available to everyone who has the desire to serve God in spirit and in truth. In the book of 1 Corinthian, chapter 15:50, it states, "Now this I say brethren, that flesh and blood cannot inherit the kingdom of God." The final mission of the Bible boot camp is to execute these orders. Matthew 28:19–20 states, "Go ye therefore, and teach all nations, baptizing them in the name of the Father, and of the Son, and of the Holy Ghost Teaching them to observe all things whatsoever I have commanded you: and lo, I am with you always, even unto the end of the world. Amen."

What a mighty God we serve. Angels bow down before Him, heaven and earth adore Him. What a mighty God we serve!

REFERENCES

Bonnell, Sutherland John. 1968. *Do You Want to Be Healed.* Harper and Row.

Chinn, Tiffani. 2004. *School Sense: How to Help Your Child Succeed in Elementary School.* Santa Monica Press.

Dunlap, Ozell S. 2006 *A Journey Worth Taking.* Tate Publishing & Enterprises.

Drucker, Peter F. 2014. *The Influential Power of Non-Verbal Communication.* Sharp Heels Group.

Fee D. Gordon, and Stuart Douglas. 1993. *How to Read the Bible for All Its Worth.* Zondervan Publishing House.

Ford, D. W. Cleverley. 1994. *Preaching the Risen Christ.* Hendrickson Publisher, Inc.

Friedman, Ian C. 2011. *Education Reform.* Published by Facts on File, Inc.

Harper, Shaun R., and Luke J. Wood. 2016. *Advancing Black Male Student Success from Preschool to PhD.* Published by Stylus Publishing.

Hickman, James J., and Dimitriy V. Masterov. 2007. *The Productive Argument for Investment in Young Children.* The National Bureau of Economic Research.

Harris, Anthony Thomas. 1969 *I'm OK—You're OK.* Harper and Rowe.

Kohn, Alfie. 2004. *What Does It Mean to Be Well-Educated?* Beacon Press.

Levin, Samuel, and Susan Engel. 2016. *A School of Our Own*. The New Press.

Liebengood, Lynn. 2016. *The Secret Place*. WestBow Press.

Mayhue, Richard. 2016. *Bible Boot Camp*. Christian Focus Production.

Money, Royce. 1987. *Ministering to Families*. Abilene Christian University Press.

Moody, Josh. 2007. *The God-Centered Life*. Regent College Publishing.

Myracle, Jared. 2014. *Common Core Standards for Parents*. John Wiley & Sons, Inc.

Pelham, Libby. 2012. *Clothing as a Form of Non-Verbal Communication*. Published by Sharp Heels Group LLC.

Sherrow, Victoria. 2011. *Education Reform*. Chelsea House.

Stodghill, Rod. 2015. *Where Everybody Looks Like Me*. Harper Collins Press.

Tye, Karen B. 2004. *Basic of Christian Education*. Chalice Press.

Villafane, Eldin. 1993. *The Liberating Spirit*. Wm. B. Eerdmans Publishing Co.

ABOUT THE AUTHOR

Rev. Dr. Ernest Branch is from Boston, Massachusetts. He has a degree in Behavioral Science from Cambridge College, a Masters from Shaw University, and a Doctorate from Newburgh Theological Seminary College. He served in The United States Marine Corps from 1956–1976, which included his time in combat in Vietnam. He is currently a pastor and grief instructor at Mt. Pilgrim Baptist Church in South Carolina.

CPSIA information can be obtained
at www.ICGtesting.com
Printed in the USA
LVHW011305181220
674522LV00011B/907